MAINTENANCE BOOK
FOR MY MOTORBIKE

DUCATI MULTISTRADA

PURCHASE

Date of purchase: _____

Purchase price: _____

Mileage at purchase: _____

Motorbike

Model: _____

Model year: _____

Registration: _____

#Engine: _____

#Châssis/VIN: _____

PHOTO OF YOUR

MOTORBIKE

Date:	Km/Miles:

Intervention: Parts changed / Repaired:

_____

_____

_____

_____

_____

_____

Notes:

_____

_____

_____

_____

$ Price _____	#Invoice _____

Service provider:

_____

_____

_____

_____

Date:	Km/Miles:

Intervention: Parts changed / Repaired:

_____

_____

_____

_____

_____

Notes:

_____

_____

_____

_____

$ Price _____	**#Invoice** _____

Service provider:

_____

_____

_____

_____

Date:	Km/Miles:

Intervention: Parts changed / Repaired:

_____
_____
_____
_____
_____
_____

Notes:

_____
_____
_____
_____

Price _____	**#Invoice** _____

Service provider:

_____
_____
_____
_____

Date:	Km/Miles:

Intervention: Parts changed / Repaired:

_____

_____

_____

_____

_____

Notes:

_____

_____

_____

_____

$ Price _____	**#Invoice** _____

Service provider:

_____

_____

_____

_____

Date:	Km/Miles:

Intervention: Parts changed / Repaired:

_____

_____

_____

_____

_____

Notes:

_____

_____

_____

_____

$ Price _____	**#Invoice** _____

Service provider:

_____

_____

_____

_____

Date:	Km/Miles:

Intervention: Parts changed / Repaired:

_____
_____
_____
_____
_____

Notes:

_____
_____
_____
_____

$ Price _____	**#Invoice** _____

Service provider:

_____
_____
_____
_____

Date:	Km/Miles:

✖ Intervention: Parts changed / Repaired:

_____
_____
_____
_____
_____

🖌 Notes:

_____
_____
_____
_____

$ Price _____	#Invoice _____

👷 Service provider:

_____
_____
_____
_____

Date:	Km/Miles:

Intervention: Parts changed / Repaired:

_____

_____

_____

_____

_____

Notes:

_____

_____

_____

_____

Price _____	**#Invoice** _____

Service provider:

_____

_____

_____

_____

Date:	Km/Miles:

Intervention: Parts changed / Repaired:

_____

_____

_____

_____

_____

Notes:

_____

_____

_____

_____

Price _____	#Invoice _____

Service provider:

_____

_____

_____

Date:	Km/Miles:

Intervention: Parts changed / Repaired:

_____

_____

_____

_____

_____

Notes:

_____

_____

_____

_____

$ Price _____	**#Invoice** _____

Service provider:

_____

_____

_____

_____

Date:	Km/Miles:

Intervention: Parts changed / Repaired:

_____

_____

_____

_____

_____

Notes:

_____

_____

_____

_____

$ Price _____	#Invoice _____

Service provider:

_____

_____

_____

_____

Date:	Km/Miles:

Intervention: Parts changed / Repaired:

_____
_____
_____
_____
_____

Notes:

_____
_____
_____
_____

$ Price _____	**#Invoice** _____

Service provider:

_____
_____
_____
_____

Date:	Km/Miles:

Intervention: Parts changed / Repaired:

_____

_____

_____

_____

_____

_____

Notes:

_____

_____

_____

_____

$ **Price** _____	**#Invoice** _____

Service provider:

_____

_____

_____

_____

Date:	Km/Miles:

Intervention: Parts changed / Repaired:

_____

_____

_____

_____

_____

Notes:

_____

_____

_____

_____

$ Price _____	**#Invoice** _____

Service provider:

_____

_____

_____

_____

Date:	Km/Miles:

Intervention: Parts changed / Repaired:

_____
_____
_____
_____
_____

Notes:

_____
_____
_____
_____

$ Price _____	**#Invoice** _____

Service provider:

_____
_____
_____
_____

Date:	Km/Miles:

Intervention: Parts changed / Repaired:

_____
_____
_____
_____
_____

Notes:

_____
_____
_____
_____

$ Price _____	**#Invoice** _____

Service provider:

_____
_____
_____
_____

Date:	Km/Miles:

Intervention: Parts changed / Repaired:

_____

_____

_____

_____

_____

Notes:

_____

_____

_____

_____

Price _____	#Invoice _____

Service provider:

_____

_____

_____

_____

Date:	Km/Miles:

Intervention: Parts changed / Repaired:

_____

_____

_____

_____

_____

Notes:

_____

_____

_____

_____

$ Price _____	**#Invoice** _____

Service provider:

_____

_____

_____

_____

Date:	Km/Miles:

Intervention: Parts changed / Repaired:

_____

_____

_____

_____

_____

Notes:

_____

_____

_____

_____

$ Price _____	**#Invoice** _____

Service provider:

_____

_____

_____

_____

Date:	Km/Miles:

⚒ Intervention: Parts changed / Repaired:

_____

_____

_____

_____

_____

_____

📐 Notes:

_____

_____

_____

_____

$ Price _____	#Invoice _____

👷 Service provider:

_____

_____

_____

_____

Date:	Km/Miles:

Intervention: Parts changed / Repaired:

_____
_____
_____
_____
_____

Notes:

_____
_____
_____
_____

Price _____	#Invoice _____

Service provider:

_____
_____
_____
_____

Date:	Km/Miles:

Intervention: Parts changed / Repaired:

_____

_____

_____

_____

_____

_____

Notes:

_____

_____

_____

_____

$ **Price** _____	**#Invoice** _____

Service provider:

_____

_____

_____

_____

Date:	Km/Miles:

Intervention: Parts changed / Repaired:

_____
_____
_____
_____
_____

Notes:

_____
_____
_____
_____

Price _____	#Invoice _____

Service provider:

_____
_____
_____

Date:	Km/Miles:

Intervention: Parts changed / Repaired:

_____

_____

_____

_____

_____

Notes:

_____

_____

_____

_____

$ Price _____	**#Invoice** _____

Service provider:

_____

_____

_____

_____

Date:	Km/Miles:

✖ Intervention: Parts changed / Repaired:

_____

_____

_____

_____

_____

✎ Notes:

_____

_____

_____

_____

$ Price _____	#Invoice _____

👷 Service provider:

_____

_____

_____

_____

Date:	Km/Miles:

Intervention: Parts changed / Repaired:

_____

_____

_____

_____

_____

_____

Notes:

_____

_____

_____

_____

$ Price _____	**#Invoice** _____

Service provider:

_____

_____

_____

_____

Date:	Km/Miles:

Intervention: Parts changed / Repaired:

_____

_____

_____

_____

_____

Notes:

_____

_____

_____

_____

Price _____	**#Invoice** _____

Service provider:

_____

_____

_____

_____

Date:	Km/Miles:

Intervention: Parts changed / Repaired:

_____

_____

_____

_____

_____

Notes:

_____

_____

_____

_____

$ Price _____	**#Invoice** _____

Service provider:

_____

_____

_____

_____

Date:	Km/Miles:

Intervention: Parts changed / Repaired:

_____

_____

_____

_____

_____

Notes:

_____

_____

_____

_____

Price _____	#Invoice _____

Service provider:

_____

_____

_____

Date:	Km/Miles:

Intervention: Parts changed / Repaired:

_____
_____
_____
_____
_____
_____

Notes:

_____
_____
_____
_____

$ Price _____	**#Invoice** _____

Service provider:

_____
_____
_____
_____

Date:	Km/Miles:

Intervention: Parts changed / Repaired:

_____

_____

_____

_____

_____

Notes:

_____

_____

_____

_____

Price _____	#Invoice _____

Service provider:

_____

_____

_____

Date:	Km/Miles:

Intervention: Parts changed / Repaired:

_____
_____
_____
_____
_____

Notes:

_____
_____
_____
_____

$ Price _____	**#Invoice** _____

Service provider:

_____
_____
_____

Date:	Km/Miles:

Intervention: Parts changed / Repaired:

_____
_____
_____
_____
_____

Notes:

_____
_____
_____
_____

Price _____	#Invoice _____

Service provider:

_____
_____
_____
_____

Date:	Km/Miles:

Intervention: Parts changed / Repaired:

_____

_____

_____

_____

_____

_____

Notes:

_____

_____

_____

_____

$ Price _____	**#Invoice** _____

Service provider:

_____

_____

_____

_____

Date:	Km/Miles:

Intervention: Parts changed / Repaired:

_____

_____

_____

_____

_____

Notes:

_____

_____

_____

_____

Price _____	**#Invoice** _____

Service provider:

_____

_____

_____

Date:	Km/Miles:

Intervention: Parts changed / Repaired:

_____

_____

_____

_____

_____

Notes:

_____

_____

_____

_____

$ Price _____	#Invoice _____

Service provider:

_____

_____

_____

_____

Date:	Km/Miles:

Intervention: Parts changed / Repaired:

_____
_____
_____
_____
_____

Notes:

_____
_____
_____
_____

Price _____	#Invoice _____

Service provider:

_____
_____
_____
_____

Date:	Km/Miles:

Intervention: Parts changed / Repaired:

_____

_____

_____

_____

_____

_____

Notes:

_____

_____

_____

_____

$ Price _____	**#Invoice** _____

Service provider:

_____

_____

_____

_____

Date:	Km/Miles:

Intervention: Parts changed / Repaired:

_____
_____
_____
_____
_____

Notes:

_____
_____
_____
_____

$ Price _____	**#Invoice** _____

Service provider:

_____
_____
_____
_____

Date:	Km/Miles:

Intervention: Parts changed / Repaired:

_____

_____

_____

_____

_____

Notes:

_____

_____

_____

_____

$ Price _____	**#Invoice** _____

Service provider:

_____

_____

_____

_____

Date:	Km/Miles:

⚒ Intervention: Parts changed / Repaired:

_____

_____

_____

_____

_____

📝 Notes:

_____

_____

_____

_____

$ Price _____	**#Invoice** _____

👷 Service provider:

_____

_____

_____

_____

Date:	Km/Miles:

✕ **Intervention: Parts changed / Repaired:**

_____
_____
_____
_____
_____

Notes:

_____
_____
_____
_____

$ **Price** _____	**#Invoice** _____

Service provider:

_____
_____
_____
_____

Date:	Km/Miles:

Intervention: Parts changed / Repaired:

_____
_____
_____
_____
_____

Notes:

_____
_____
_____
_____

$ Price _____	**#Invoice** _____

Service provider:

_____
_____
_____
_____

Date:	Km/Miles:

Intervention: Parts changed / Repaired:

_____

_____

_____

_____

_____

Notes:

_____

_____

_____

_____

$ Price _____	**#Invoice** _____

Service provider:

_____

_____

_____

_____

Date:	Km/Miles:

✕ Intervention: Parts changed / Repaired:

_____

_____

_____

_____

_____

📝 Notes:

_____

_____

_____

_____

💲 Price _____	#Invoice _____

👷 Service provider:

_____

_____

_____

Date:	Km/Miles:

Intervention: Parts changed / Repaired:

_____

_____

_____

_____

_____

Notes:

_____

_____

_____

_____

$ Price _____	#Invoice _____

Service provider:

_____

_____

_____

_____

Date:	Km/Miles:

Intervention: Parts changed / Repaired:

_____
_____
_____
_____
_____

Notes:

_____
_____
_____
_____

Price _____	#Invoice _____

Service provider:

_____
_____
_____
_____

Date:	Km/Miles:

Intervention: Parts changed / Repaired:

_____

_____

_____

_____

_____

Notes:

_____

_____

_____

_____

Price _____	**#Invoice** _____

Service provider:

_____

_____

_____

_____

Date:	Km/Miles:

⚒ Intervention: Parts changed / Repaired:

_____

_____

_____

_____

_____

📝 Notes:

_____

_____

_____

_____

💲 Price _____	#Invoice _____

👷 Service provider:

_____

_____

_____

_____

Date:	Km/Miles:

Intervention: Parts changed / Repaired:

_____

_____

_____

_____

_____

Notes:

_____

_____

_____

_____

$ Price _____	#Invoice _____

Service provider:

_____

_____

_____

_____

Date:	Km/Miles:

Intervention: Parts changed / Repaired:

_____
_____
_____
_____
_____

Notes:

_____
_____
_____
_____

Price _____	#Invoice _____

Service provider:

_____
_____
_____
_____

Date:	Km/Miles:

⚒ Intervention: Parts changed / Repaired:

_____

_____

_____

_____

_____

📝 Notes:

_____

_____

_____

_____

$ Price _____	**#Invoice** _____

👷 Service provider:

_____

_____

_____

_____

Date:	Km/Miles:

✖ Intervention: Parts changed / Repaired:

_____
_____
_____
_____
_____

📝 Notes:

_____
_____
_____
_____

$ Price _____	#Invoice _____

👷 Service provider:

_____
_____
_____
_____

Date:	Km/Miles:

⚒ Intervention: Parts changed / Repaired:

_____

_____

_____

_____

_____

✎ Notes:

_____

_____

_____

_____

$ Price _____	**#Invoice** _____

👷 Service provider:

_____

_____

_____

_____

Date:

Km/Miles:

Intervention: Parts changed / Repaired:

_____
_____
_____
_____
_____

Notes:

_____
_____
_____
_____

Price _____

#Invoice _____

Service provider:

_____
_____
_____
_____

Date:	Km/Miles:

⚒ Intervention: Parts changed / Repaired:

_____
_____
_____
_____
_____

📝 Notes:

_____
_____
_____
_____

$ Price _____	**#Invoice** _____

👷 Service provider:

_____
_____
_____
_____

Date:	Km/Miles:

Intervention: Parts changed / Repaired:

_____

_____

_____

_____

_____

Notes:

_____

_____

_____

_____

Price _____	#Invoice _____

Service provider:

_____

_____

_____

Date:	Km/Miles:

⚒ Intervention: Parts changed / Repaired:

_____

_____

_____

_____

_____

📝 Notes:

_____

_____

_____

_____

$ Price _____	**#Invoice** _____

👷 Service provider:

_____

_____

_____

Date:	Km/Miles:

Intervention: Parts changed / Repaired:

_____

_____

_____

_____

_____

Notes:

_____

_____

_____

_____

Price _____	#Invoice _____

Service provider:

_____

_____

_____

_____

Date:	Km/Miles:

✕ Intervention: Parts changed / Repaired:

_____

_____

_____

_____

_____

✎ Notes:

_____

_____

_____

_____

$ Price _____	**#Invoice** _____

Service provider:

_____

_____

_____

Date:	Km/Miles:

Intervention: Parts changed / Repaired:

_____

_____

_____

_____

_____

Notes:

_____

_____

_____

_____

Price _____	**#Invoice** _____

Service provider:

_____

_____

_____

_____

Date:	Km/Miles:

✖ Intervention: Parts changed / Repaired:

_____

_____

_____

_____

_____

✎ Notes:

_____

_____

_____

_____

$ Price _____	**#Invoice** _____

☺ Service provider:

_____

_____

_____

Date:	Km/Miles:

Intervention: Parts changed / Repaired:

_____

_____

_____

_____

_____

Notes:

_____

_____

_____

_____

Price _____	**#Invoice** _____

Service provider:

_____

_____

_____

_____

Date:	Km/Miles:

Intervention: Parts changed / Repaired:

_____

_____

_____

_____

_____

Notes:

_____

_____

_____

_____

Price _____	**#Invoice** _____

Service provider:

_____

_____

_____

Date:	Km/Miles:

Intervention: Parts changed / Repaired:

_____
_____
_____
_____
_____
_____

Notes:

_____
_____
_____
_____

Price _____	**#Invoice** _____

Service provider:

_____
_____
_____
_____

Date:	Km/Miles:

Intervention: Parts changed / Repaired:

_____

_____

_____

_____

_____

Notes:

_____

_____

_____

_____

Price _____	**#Invoice** _____

Service provider:

_____

_____

_____

_____

Date:	Km/Miles:

Intervention: Parts changed / Repaired:

_____

_____

_____

_____

_____

Notes:

_____

_____

_____

_____

Price _____	#Invoice _____

Service provider:

_____

_____

_____

_____

Date:	Km/Miles:

Intervention: Parts changed / Repaired:

_____

_____

_____

_____

_____

Notes:

_____

_____

_____

_____

$ Price _____	**#Invoice** _____

Service provider:

_____

_____

_____

_____

Date:	Km/Miles:

Intervention: Parts changed / Repaired:

_____

_____

_____

_____

_____

Notes:

_____

_____

_____

_____

$ Price _____	#Invoice _____

Service provider:

_____

_____

_____

_____

Date:	Km/Miles:

⚒ Intervention: Parts changed / Repaired:

_____

_____

_____

_____

_____

✎ Notes:

_____

_____

_____

_____

$ Price _____	**#Invoice** _____

👷 Service provider:

_____

_____

_____

_____

Date:	Km/Miles:

Intervention: Parts changed / Repaired:

_____
_____
_____
_____
_____

Notes:

_____
_____
_____
_____

Price _____	#Invoice _____

Service provider:

_____
_____
_____

Date:	Km/Miles:

Intervention: Parts changed / Repaired:

_____

_____

_____

_____

_____

Notes:

_____

_____

_____

_____

Price _____	**#Invoice** _____

Service provider:

_____

_____

_____

_____

Date:	Km/Miles:

Intervention: Parts changed / Repaired:

_____
_____
_____
_____
_____

Notes:

_____
_____
_____
_____

Price _____	#Invoice _____

Service provider:

_____
_____
_____

Date:	Km/Miles:

Intervention: Parts changed / Repaired:

_____

_____

_____

_____

_____

Notes:

_____

_____

_____

_____

$ Price _____	**#Invoice** _____

Service provider:

_____

_____

_____

_____

Date:	Km/Miles:

Intervention: Parts changed / Repaired:

_____

_____

_____

_____

_____

Notes:

_____

_____

_____

_____

Price _____	#Invoice _____

Service provider:

_____

_____

_____

Date:	Km/Miles:

⚒ Intervention: Parts changed / Repaired:

_____

_____

_____

_____

_____

📝 Notes:

_____

_____

_____

_____

$ Price _____	**#Invoice** _____

👷 Service provider:

_____

_____

_____

_____

Date:	Km/Miles:

Intervention: Parts changed / Repaired:

_____
_____
_____
_____
_____

Notes:

_____
_____
_____
_____

Price _____	**#Invoice** _____

Service provider:

_____
_____
_____

Date:	Km/Miles:

⚒ Intervention: Parts changed / Repaired:

_____

_____

_____

_____

_____

📝 Notes:

_____

_____

_____

_____

$ Price _____	**#Invoice** _____

👷 Service provider:

_____

_____

_____

_____

Date:	Km/Miles:

Intervention: Parts changed / Repaired:

_____
_____
_____
_____
_____

Notes:

_____
_____
_____
_____

Price _____	**#Invoice** _____

Service provider:

_____
_____
_____
_____

Date:	Km/Miles:

Intervention: Parts changed / Repaired:

_____
_____
_____
_____
_____

Notes:

_____
_____
_____
_____

$ Price _____	**#Invoice** _____

Service provider:

_____
_____
_____
_____

Date:	Km/Miles:

✖ Intervention: Parts changed / Repaired:

_____

_____

_____

_____

_____

📝 Notes:

_____

_____

_____

_____

$ Price _____	#Invoice _____

👷 Service provider:

_____

_____

_____

_____

Date:	Km/Miles:

Intervention: Parts changed / Repaired:

_____
_____
_____
_____
_____
_____

Notes:

_____
_____
_____
_____

$ Price _____	#Invoice _____

Service provider:

_____
_____
_____
_____

Date:	Km/Miles:

⚒ Intervention: Parts changed / Repaired:

_____
_____
_____
_____
_____

📝 Notes:

_____
_____
_____
_____

💲 Price _____	#Invoice _____

👷 Service provider:

_____
_____
_____

Date:	Km/Miles:

Intervention: Parts changed / Repaired:

_____
_____
_____
_____
_____

Notes:

_____
_____
_____
_____

$ Price _____	**#Invoice** _____

Service provider:

_____
_____
_____
_____

Date:	Km/Miles:

Intervention: Parts changed / Repaired:

_____
_____
_____
_____
_____

Notes:

_____
_____
_____
_____

Price _____	#Invoice _____

Service provider:

_____
_____
_____
_____

Date:	Km/Miles:

Intervention: Parts changed / Repaired:

_____

_____

_____

_____

_____

Notes:

_____

_____

_____

_____

$ Price _____	**#Invoice** _____

Service provider:

_____

_____

_____

_____

Date:	Km/Miles:

Intervention: Parts changed / Repaired:

_____

_____

_____

_____

_____

Notes:

_____

_____

_____

_____

$ Price _____	**#Invoice** _____

Service provider:

_____

_____

_____

Date:	Km/Miles:

Intervention: Parts changed / Repaired:

_____

_____

_____

_____

_____

Notes:

_____

_____

_____

_____

$ Price _____	**#Invoice** _____

Service provider:

_____

_____

_____

_____

Date:	Km/Miles:

Intervention: Parts changed / Repaired:

_____
_____
_____
_____
_____

Notes:

_____
_____
_____
_____

Price _____	#Invoice _____

Service provider:

_____
_____
_____
_____

Date:	Km/Miles:

⚒ Intervention: Parts changed / Repaired:

_____

_____

_____

_____

_____

✎ Notes:

_____

_____

_____

_____

$ Price _____	**#Invoice** _____

👷 Service provider:

_____

_____

_____

_____

Date:	Km/Miles:

Intervention: Parts changed / Repaired:

_____

_____

_____

_____

_____

Notes:

_____

_____

_____

_____

Price _____	#Invoice _____

Service provider:

_____

_____

_____

_____

Date:	Km/Miles:

Intervention: Parts changed / Repaired:

_____

_____

_____

_____

_____

Notes:

_____

_____

_____

_____

Price _____	#Invoice _____

Service provider:

_____

_____

_____

_____

Date:	Km/Miles:

⚒ Intervention: Parts changed / Repaired:

_____

_____

_____

_____

_____

📝 Notes:

_____

_____

_____

_____

$ Price _____	**#Invoice** _____

👷 Service provider:

_____

_____

_____

_____

Date:	Km/Miles:

Intervention: Parts changed / Repaired:

_____

_____

_____

_____

_____

Notes:

_____

_____

_____

_____

Price _____	#Invoice _____

Service provider:

_____

_____

_____

_____

Date:	Km/Miles:

Intervention: Parts changed / Repaired:

_____

_____

_____

_____

_____

_____

Notes:

_____

_____

_____

_____

$ Price _____	**#Invoice** _____

Service provider:

_____

_____

_____

_____

Date:	Km/Miles:

Intervention: Parts changed / Repaired:

_____

_____

_____

_____

_____

Notes:

_____

_____

_____

_____

Price _____	**#Invoice** _____

Service provider:

_____

_____

_____

_____

Date:	Km/Miles:

Intervention: Parts changed / Repaired:

_____

_____

_____

_____

_____

Notes:

_____

_____

_____

_____

Price _____	**#Invoice** _____

Service provider:

_____

_____

_____

_____

Adress Book

Made in the USA
Las Vegas, NV
27 February 2022

44684543R00057